Paintings by African-Americans

from the collection of the
National Museum of American Art

Smithsonian Institution   **A Book of Postcards**

This book is published in cooperation with the Smithsonian Institution's
National Museum of American Art by Pomegranate Artbooks, Box 808022, Petaluma, CA 94975

ISBN 0-87654-748-X
Pomegranate Catalog No. A570

Pomegranate publishes several other postcard collections on many different subjects.
Please write to the publisher for more information.

Cover design by Nicholas Valentine
© 1991 Smithsonian Institution
Printed in Korea

The National Museum of American Art, Smithsonian Institution, is dedicated to the preservation, exhibition, and study of the visual arts in America. The museum, whose publications program also includes the scholarly journal *American Art*, has extensive research resources: the databases of the Inventories of American Painting and Sculpture, several image archives, and a variety of scholarly fellowships. For more information or a catalogue of publications, write: Office of Publications, National Museum of American Art, Smithsonian Institution, Washington, DC 20560.

The National Museum of American Art houses the finest collection of works by African-American artists of any general museum today. More than 1,500 diverse objects in a variety of media are represented, from portraiture of the early republic to the creative expressions of contemporary men and women. The collection reflects European styles and subjects in the eighteenth and nineteenth centuries, explorations of social and anecdotal aspects of black culture in the 1920s and 1930s, experiments with color and abstract form in recent years, and throughout, moving examples of self-taught expression.

The artists include:

Edward Mitchell Bannister, Frederick Brown, Claude Clark, Allan Rohan Crite, Emilio Cruz, Sam Gilliam, Malvin Gray Johnson, William H. Johnson, Loïs Mailou Jones, Jacob Lawrence, Charles Searles, Henry O. Tanner, Alma Thomas, and Bob Thompson.

Paintings by African-Americans

LOÏS MAILOU JONES (born 1906) studied in Paris in
the late 1930s while on a sabbatical from Howard
University. Her illustrations, textile designs, and
paintings incorporate theories of modern art and motifs
drawn from African and other cultures.

Pomegranate • Box 808022 • Petaluma, CA 94975

Les Fetiches, 1938
Oil on canvas, 25½ x 21 in.
National Museum of American Art, Smithsonian Institution
Museum purchase made possible by Mrs. N. H. Green,
Dr. R. Harlan and Francis Musgrave, 1990.56

Paintings by African-Americans

WILLIAM H. JOHNSON (1901–1970) studied art in New
York and lived in France, Denmark and Norway. Upon
returning to the United States in 1938, he began painting
images of African-American life, drawing on both his youth
in rural South Carolina and life in New York City where he
lived in the 1930s and 40s.

Pomegranate • Box 808022 • Petaluma, CA 94975

Sweet Adeline, c. 1940
Tempera, pen and ink with pencil on paper, 15¼ x 12½ in.
National Museum of American Art, Smithsonian Institution
Gift of the Harmon Foundation, 1967.59.147
© Smithsonian Institution

Paintings by African-Americans

ALMA WOODSEY THOMAS (1896–1978) established
herself as an artist despite having to overcome obstacles of
racism and sexism. She was welcomed into the circle of
Washington, D.C., Color School painters, a group whose
paintings earned international attention in the 1960s.

Pomegranate • Box 808022 • Petaluma, CA 94975

Atmospheric Effects II, 1971
Watercolor, 22 x 30 in.
National Museum of American Art, Smithsonian Institution
Gift of Vincent Melzac, 1976.140.4

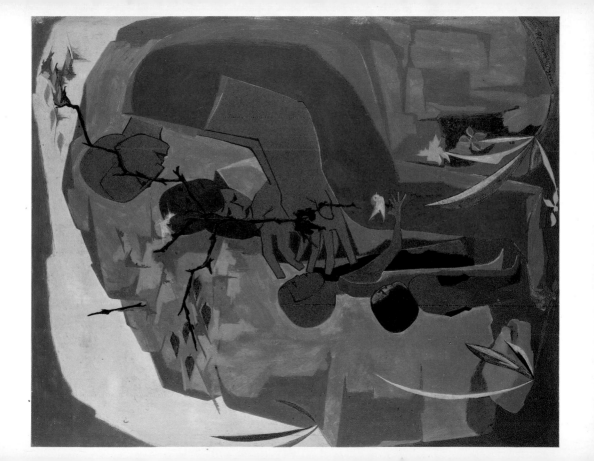

Paintings by African-Americans

JACOB LAWRENCE (born 1917) began his career on the
Federal Art Project of the Works Progress Administration
in New York. In prints, drawings, and paintings, he has
devoted his career to representing the history and culture
of the African-American community.

Pomegranate • Box 808022 • Petaluma, CA 94975

"Men Exist for the Sake of One Another.
Teach Them Then or Bear With Them."
(from the series *Great Ideas of Western Man*), 1958
Oil on masonite, 20¾ x 16¾ in.
National Museum of American Art, Smithsonian Institution
Gift of the Container Corporation of America, 1984.124.171

Paintings by African-Americans

HENRY OSSAWA TANNER (1859–1937) moved to Paris in 1891 so that he could paint without the pressures of racial discrimination in the United States. He traveled throughout Europe and the Holy Land painting many religious scenes.

Pomegranate • Box 808022 • Petaluma, CA 94975

Street Scene, Tangier, 1910
Oil on paperboard, 10⅝ x 13¾ in.
National Museum of American Art, Smithsonian Institution
Gift of Mr. and Mrs. Norman B. Robbins, 1983.95.196A
© Smithsonian Institution

Paintings by African-Americans

EMILIO CRUZ (born 1938) paints in an expressive style
inspired by imagined events and the history of Africa and
the New World.

Pomegranate • Box 808022 • Petaluma, CA 94975

Figurative Composition #7, 1965
Oil on canvas, 59¼ x 67 in.
National Museum of American Art, Smithsonian Institution
Gift of Mr. and Mrs. David K. Anderson,
Martha Jackson Memorial, 1980.137.21
© Smithsonian Institution

Paintings by African-Americans

MALVIN GRAY JOHNSON (1896–1934) was active during
the heyday of the Harlem Renaissance of the 1930s. He
simplified the forms of his subjects and occasionally
emphasized his African past by including African imagery
in his paintings.

Pomegranate • Box 808022 • Petaluma, CA 94975

Brothers, 1934
Oil on canvas, 38 x 30⅛ in.
National Museum of American Art, Smithsonian Institution
Gift of the Harmon Foundation, 1967.59.29

Paintings by African-Americans

JACOB LAWRENCE (born 1917) began his career on the
Federal Art Project of the Works Progress Administration
in New York. In prints, drawings, and paintings, he has
devoted his career to representing the history and culture
of the African-American community.

Pomegranate • Box 808022 • Petaluma, CA 94975

New Jersey (from the *United States Series*), 1946
Watercolor, gouache and pencil on paper, 24⅛ x 20$^{1}/_{16}$ in.
National Museum of American Art, Smithsonian Institution
Gift of the Container Corporation of America, 1984.124.172
© Smithsonian Institution

Paintings by African-Americans

SAM GILLIAM (born 1933) moved to Washington, D.C. in
1962 and was influenced by the Washington Color School
painters. Through his teaching and encouragement of
younger artists, Gilliam has demonstrated his dedication to
the next generation of artists.

Pomegranate • Box 808022 • Petaluma, CA 94975

Open Cylinder, 1979
Oil on canvas, 81 x 35½ in.
National Museum of American Art, Smithsonian Institution
Gift of Mr. and Mrs. Albert Ritzenberg, 1981.165A,B

Paintings by African-Americans

WILLIAM H. JOHNSON (1901–1970) studied art in New
York and lived in France, Denmark and Norway. Upon
returning to the United States in 1938, he began painting
images of African-American life, drawing on both his youth
in rural South Carolina and life in New York City where he
lived in the 1930s and 40s.

Pomegranate • Box 808022 • Petaluma, CA 94975

Untitled (Soapbox Racing), c. 1939–40
Tempera, pen and ink on paper, 14⅛ x 17⅞ in.
National Museum of American Art, Smithsonian Institution
Gift of the Harmon Foundation, 1967.59.160

Paintings by African-Americans

CLAUDE CLARK (born 1915) has taught art since 1948 in Alabama and California and continues to research the roots of African-American art in Africa, specifically Ghana and Egypt.

Pomegranate • Box 808022 • Petaluma, CA 94975

Resting, 1944
Oil on canvas, 30 x 25 in.
National Museum of American Art, Smithsonian Institution
Gift of the Harmon Foundation, 1967.57.32
© Smithsonian Institution

Paintings by African-Americans

ALMA WOODSEY THOMAS (1896–1978) established
herself as an artist despite having to overcome obstacles of
racism and sexism. She was welcomed into the circle of
Washington, D.C., Color School painters, a group whose
paintings earned international attention in the 1960s.

Pomegranate • Box 808022 • Petaluma, CA 94975

Red Abstraction, 1959
Oil on canvas, 40 x 27¾ in.
National Museum of American Art, Smithsonian Institution
Gift of the Artist, 1978.40.2
© Smithsonian Institution

Paintings by African-Americans

WILLIAM H. JOHNSON (1901–1970) studied art in New York and lived in France, Denmark and Norway. Upon returning to the United States in 1938, he began painting images of African-American life, drawing on both his youth in rural South Carolina and life in New York City where he lived in the 1930s and 40s.

Pomegranate • Box 808022 • Petaluma, CA 94975

Going to Market, c. 1940
Oil on wood, 34⅛ x 34⅞ in.
National Museum of American Art, Smithsonian Institution
Gift of the Harmon Foundation, 1967.59.591
© Smithsonian Institution

Paintings by African-Americans

EMILIO CRUZ (born 1938) paints in an expressive style
inspired by imagined events and the history of Africa and
the New World.

Pomegranate • Box 808022 • Petaluma, CA 94975

The Dance, 1962
Oil on paper, 21⅞ x 30⅝ in.
National Museum of American Art, Smithsonian Institution
Gift of Virginia Zabriskie, 1979.113.1

Paintings by African-Americans

JACOB LAWRENCE (born 1917) began his career on the
Federal Art Project of the Works Progress Administration
in New York. In prints, drawings, and paintings, he has
devoted his career to representing the history and culture
of the African-American community.

Pomegranate • Box 808022 • Petaluma, CA 94975

Dreams No. 2, 1965
Tempera on fiberboard, 35¾ x 24 in.
National Museum of American Art, Smithsonian Institution
Gift of The Sara Roby Foundation, 1986.6.95

Paintings by African-Americans

CHARLES SEARLES (born 1937) studied art in his
hometown of Philadelphia. The mural *Celebration* was
commissioned by the federal government's Art-in-
Architecture program for the William J. Green, Jr. Federal
Building in Philadelphia.

Pomegranate • Box 808022 • Petaluma, CA 94975

Celebration (detail), 1975
Acrylic on canvas, 27½ x 81⅝ in.
National Museum of American Art, Smithsonian Institution
Transfer from General Services Administration, 1977.47.31
© Smithsonian Institution

Paintings by African-Americans

WILLIAM H. JOHNSON (1901–1970) studied art in New York and lived in France, Denmark and Norway. Upon returning to the United States in 1938, he began painting images of African-American life, drawing on both his youth in rural South Carolina and life in New York City where he lived in the 1930s and 40s.

Pomegranate • Box 808022 • Petaluma, CA 94975

Soldiers Dancing, c. 1942
Gouache, pen and ink with pencil on paper, 15⅛ x 19¾ in.
National Museum of American Art, Smithsonian Institution
Gift of the Harmon Foundation, 1967.59.162

Paintings by African-Americans

ALLAN ROHAN CRITE (born 1910) painted local scenes of
Boston while employed by the Federal Art Project of the
Works Progress Administration.

Pomegranate • Box 808022 • Petaluma, CA 94975

School's Out, 1936
Oil on canvas, 30¼ x 36⅛ in.
National Museum of American Art, Smithsonian Institution
Transfer from The Museum of Modern Art, 1971.447.18
© Smithsonian Institution

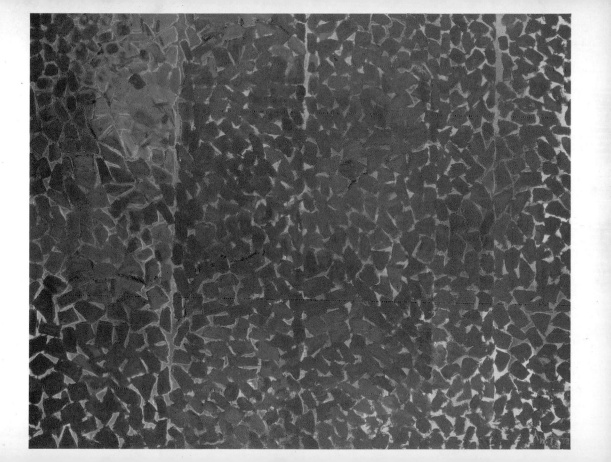

Paintings by African-Americans

ALMA WOODSEY THOMAS (1896–1978) established
herself as an artist despite having to overcome obstacles of
racism and sexism. She was welcomed into the circle of
Washington, D.C., Color School painters, a group whose
paintings earned international attention in the 1960s.

Pomegranate • Box 808022 • Petaluma, CA 94975

Autumn Leaves Fluttering in the Breeze, 1973
Acrylic on canvas, 40 x 50 in.
National Museum of American Art, Smithsonian Institution
Gift of the Artist, 1980.36.9

Paintings by African-Americans

JACOB LAWRENCE (born 1917) began his career on the
Federal Art Project of the Works Progress Administration
in New York. In prints, drawings, and paintings, he has
devoted his career to representing the history and culture
of the African-American community.

Pomegranate • Box 808022 • Petaluma, CA 94975

Community (Study for Mural, Jamaica, NY), 1986
Gouache on paper, 30 x 22⅛ in.
National Museum of American Art, Smithsonian Institution
Transfer from the General Services Administration,
Art-in-Architecture Program, 1990.36

Paintings by African-Americans

MALVIN GRAY JOHNSON (1896–1934) was active during
the heyday of the Harlem Renaissance of the 1930s. He
simplified the forms of his subjects and occasionally
emphasized his African past by including African imagery
in his paintings.

Pomegranate • Box 808022 • Petaluma, CA 94975

Self Portrait, 1934
Oil on canvas, 38⅛ x 30 in.
National Museum of American Art, Smithsonian Institution
Gift of the Harmon Foundation, 1967.57.30

Paintings by African-Americans

SAM GILLIAM (born 1933) moved to Washington, D.C., in 1962 and was influenced by the Washington Color School painters. Through his teaching and encouragement of younger artists, Gilliam has demonstrated his dedication to the next generation of artists.

Pomegranate • Box 808022 • Petaluma, CA 94975

In Celebration, 1987
Serigraph on paper, 30½ x 38¼ in.
National Museum of American Art, Smithsonian Institution
Gift of Smithsonian Institution Resident
Associate Program, 1987.54
© Smithsonian Institution

Paintings by African-Americans

EDWARD MITCHELL BANNISTER (1828 Canada–1901 USA)
created a sensation when one of his paintings won first prize
at the Philadelphia Centennial Exposition in 1876. He was also
a respected and knowledgeable art critic.

Pomegranate • Box 808022 • Petaluma, CA 94975

Seaweed Gatherers, 1898
Oil on canvas, 24 x 19⅞ in.
National Museum of American Art, Smithsonian Institution
Gift of H. Alan and Melvin Frank, 1983.95.149

Paintings by African-Americans

HENRY OSSAWA TANNER (1859–1937) moved to Paris in 1891 so that he could paint without the pressures of racial discrimination in the United States. He traveled throughout Europe and the Holy Land painting many religious scenes.

Pomegranate • Box 808022 • Petaluma, CA 94975

Fishermen at Sea, 1913
Oil on canvas, 46 x 35¼ in.
National Museum of American Art, Smithsonian Institution
Gift of Jesse O. Tanner, 1983.95.215

Paintings by African-Americans

JACOB LAWRENCE (born 1917) began his career on the
Federal Art Project of the Works Progress Administration
in New York. In prints, drawings, and paintings, he has
devoted his career to representing the history and culture
of the African-American community.

Pomegranate • Box 808022 • Petaluma, CA 94975

*"In a Free Government, the Security of Civil Rights Must be the
Same as that for Religious . . ."* (Great Idea Series), 1976
Opaque watercolor and pencil on paper, 28¾ x 21⅜ in.
National Museum of American Art, Smithsonian Institution
Gift of the Container Corporation of America, 1984.124.170
© Smithsonian Institution

Paintings by African-Americans

EMILIO CRUZ (born 1938) paints in an expressive style
inspired by imagined events and the history of Africa and
the New World.

Pomegranate • Box 808022 • Petaluma, CA 94975

Angola's Dreams Grasp Fingertips, 1973
Acrylic on canvas, 84⅛ x 84 in.
National Museum of American Art, Smithsonian Institution
Gift of Mr. and Mrs. David K. Anderson,
Martha Jackson Memorial, 1980.137.20
© Smithsonian Institution

Paintings by African-Americans

FREDERICK BROWN (born 1945) grew up on Chicago's
South Side. His portraits celebrate those who have made
important contributions to contemporary culture.

Pomegranate • Box 808022 • Petaluma, CA 94975

Junior Wells, 1989
Oil on linen, 36 x 30 in.
National Museum of American Art, Smithsonian Institution
Museum purchase made possible by
Wm. Cost Johnson, George Story,
Robert J. Oliver and Grette Wagner-Barwig, 1990.31

Paintings by African-Americans

LOÏS MAILOU JONES (born 1905) studied in Paris in
the late 1930s while on a sabbatical from Howard
University. Her illustrations, textile designs, and
paintings incorporate theories of modern art and motifs
drawn from African and other cultures.

Pomegranate • Box 808022 • Petaluma, CA 94975

Jardin du Luxembourg, c. 1938
Oil on canvas, 23¾ x 28¾ in.
National Museum of American Art, Smithsonian Institution
Gift of Gladys P. Payne in honor of Alice P. Moore, 1990.7
© Smithsonian Institution

Paintings by African-Americans

BOB THOMPSON (1937–1966) moved from Kentucky to
New York, where he established his personal style of
brightly colored expressionist paintings. Many of his works
reflect the influence and subject matter of the European
masters.

Pomegranate • Box 808022 • Petaluma, CA 94975

Enchanted Rider, 1962–63
Oil on canvas, 62¾ x 46⅞ in.
National Museum of American Art, Smithsonian Institution
Gift of Mr. and Mrs. David K. Anderson,
Martha Jackson Memorial, 1975.21
© Smithsonian Institution

Paintings by African-Americans

JACOB LAWRENCE (born 1917) began his career on the
Federal Art Project of the Works Progress Administration
in New York. In prints, drawings, and paintings, he has
devoted his career to representing the history and culture
of the African-American community.

Pomegranate • Box 808022 • Petaluma, CA 94975

The Library, 1960
Tempera on fiberboard, 24 x 29⅞ in.
National Museum of American Art, Smithsonian Institution
Gift of S. C. Johnson & Son, Inc., 1969.47.24